Lorikeet's Festive Celebration
Second Edition

Rainbow Lorikeets are so full of life, their fun-loving, mischievous nature is captivating.

This story, the eighth in the Lorikeet's Book Series for young readers, is based on a family of Lorikeets who, when they visit the garden today, find it decorated and a delicious selection of food available. All their friends who have visited before drop in.

Through my words and the creative vision of Lillian Falzon, whose illustrations brought these characters to life, I hope you enjoy a peek into the adventures of this quirky, colourful family.

It's a crisp, fresh morning. The Kookaburra's are laughing in the distance greeting the new day.

The rooster starts his loud "cock-a-doodle-doo" waking the geese, the cows, chickens and the resident humans.

The noisy Rainbow Lorikeet families fly into the garden in a cloud of green, yellow, red and blue. Anyone who isn't awake will be very soon.

Today in the garden there is something wonderfully different. The Rainbow Lorikeets find the trees and bushes have been decorated with tinsel and baubles.

Expecting the usual sunflower seed in trays, they find an array of delicious delights on offer: sunflower seeds, honey-soaked bread, nectar mix and fresh fruit.

A larger bird bath with sparkling clean water has been added.

The fabulous aroma of the food excites their taste buds so much, the Lorikeets forget to look around to check the safety of the area and instead of waiting in the trees they fly directly to the trays where the resident human is still serving the delicious delights.

Lawrence and Loretta and their family of Rainbow Lorikeets are joined by: King Royce; Rosanna, the Lorikeet Queen; and their family of Lorikeet Princes and Princesses.

When King Royce sees the amazing spread, he asks his Princes: Rory and Ryan to fly away and personally invite their cousins and relatives.

Within minutes the Princes return followed by other
Rainbow Lorikeet families and two special visitors, who
only come to the garden a few times a year.

These special visitors, Peter and Penelope the Pale
Headed Rosellas, have dressed up for the occasion with
pale yellow caps, white beaks, blue cheeks, dusty blue
cloaks with black shoulders and long blue coat tails.

The pale shirts are enhanced by festive neck wear.

Peter and Penelope look around with their silky black eyes, they find a tray and settle in to enjoy the feast.

Unlike Rainbow Lorikeets, the Pale Headed Rosella's are calm and quiet and eat without the chatter and rambunctiousness.

Stewart and his family of Scaly-breasted Lorikeets fly in with their green and yellow colours on display. Now there are more than one hundred birds in the once peaceful garden.

All of the singing, chirping, screeching and the birds flying from tray to tray make it very festive.

Colin the Cockatoo arrives with a loud screech, his white wings with pale yellow lining outstretched, he swoops over a tray and scares the Lorikeets.

He settles on a tray and waves his head from side to side, displaying his yellow plume. Some of the Lorikeets fly back to the tray and join him.

Colin doesn't mind having company today and settles in to enjoy the honey-soaked bread, fruit and seeds with his newfound friends, eating as per his ritual, looking around, picking up the food and then eating.

On the ground there are many Lorikeets eating the seeds that have dropped and in amongst them are Peaceful Doves quietly sharing the feast.

Several Lorikeets are drinking water from the bird bath, others lay in the water, flap their wings and splash water over their back and head having a great time.

After the bath fun, the Lorikeet's stretch out their wings, shake and preen one another while patiently waiting for an available tray.

Suddenly! The garden is bare as birds flutter around in fear. They squawk and screech and fly into the trees.

Below, lurching his way through the garden, not aware of this festive occasion, is Gustav Goanna in his usual suave grey outfit.

Today Gustav is not interested in climbing trees to feast on eggs or birds, he is on his way to the dam to see if any frogs or other small, tasty treats are hanging around the waters' edge.

Once Gustav passes through, King Royce lets out a screech and the birds return to the trays and to the ground to continue the wonderful feast.

Several Lorikeets fly to the tray where Lawrence and Loretta are eating.

Lawrence, not impressed, puffs up his chest and begins to lurch forward when King Royce screeches, reminding Lawrence of the promise to keep peace and harmony in the garden.

Lawrence calms himself, remembers his promise to King Royce and invites others to share his tray.

By mid-morning everyone has had their fill. The delicious delights have all been eaten.

The furry beasts, Gina the Labradoodle and Johnson the Stumpy Tail Cattle dog have joined the party and are sniffing the ground for leftovers.

The Rainbow Lorikeets, the Pale Headed Rosellas, the Scaly-breasted Lorikeets, Colin the Cockatoo and the Peaceful Doves all fly away into the distance chirping, screeching and chattering, thanking the resident human for such a wonderful spread and this special celebration.

Lorikeet's Festive Celebration

ISBN

978-1-7642196-5-5 (Paperback)

978-1-7642196-6-2 (eBook)